**Geoff Thompson's Ground Fighting Series**

# Fighting From Your Back

# Geoff Thompson

SUMMERSDALE

Summersdale Publishers Ltd
46 West Street
Chichester
West Sussex
PO19 1RP
United Kingdom

www.summersdale.com

Printed and bound in Great Britain.

ISBN 1 84024 174 8

Photographs by Paul Raynor

## Important note

With ground fighting techniques the author recommends that you practice only under supervision to avoid accidents and always employ the 'tap system' in practice (if you want to submit or a technique is too painful or you wish to stop practice at any time tap the mat, tap yourself or your opponent with your hand or foot; if this is not possible just say to your opponent 'tap'). If an opponent taps out it is imperative that you release your hold immediately or suffer the consequence of what might be serious injury, and remember, what goes around comes around. If you do not release when he taps he may not release the next time you tap.

If you have or believe you may have a medical condition the techniques outlined in this book should not be attempted without first consulting your doctor. Some of the techniques in this book require a high level of fitness and suppleness and should not be attempted by someone lacking such fitness. The author and the publishers cannot accept any responsibility for any proceedings or prosecutions brought or instituted against any person or body as a result of the use or misuse of any techniques described in this book or any loss, injury or damage caused thereby.

# About the author

Geoff Thompson has written over 20 published books and is known world wide for his autobiography *Watch My back*, about his nine years working as a night club doorman. He holds the rank of 6th Dan black belt in Japanese karate, 1st Dan in Judo and is also qualified to senior instructor level in various other forms of wrestling and martial arts. He has several scripts for stage, screen and TV in development with Destiny Films.

He has published several articles for GQ magazine, and has also been featured in *FHM*, *Maxim*, *Arena*, *Front* and *Loaded* magazines, and has been featured many times on mainstream TV.

Geoff is currently a contributing editor for *Men's Fitness* magazine.

For full details of other books and videos by Geoff Thompson, visit www.geoffthompson.com

## ACKNOWLEDGEMENTS

With special thanks to Marc McFann and my good friend and grappling sempai Rick Young.

# Contents

Introduction                                                      8

Chapter One
The Guards                                                        21

Chapter Two
Attacking from your back                                          27

Chapter Three
Chokes and Strangles                                             37

Chapter Four
Chokes and Strangles from under the scarf hold        54

Chapter Five
Bars from your back                                              64

Chapter Six
Finger and wrist locks                                           72

Chapter Seven
Drilling                                                              80

Conclusion                                                         88

# Introduction

Since time immemorial, being on your back in a real fight has been, it would seem, synonymous with defeat. The person underneath is only seconds away from being beaten by the assailant on top. In the majority of cases the synonym was correct. Being pinned on your back (unless you are a trained ground fighter) is the final pre-cursor to defeat, even to a trained ground fighter it is still not the favoured position, though it is certainly not the coup de grace.

If you study a good Judoka he will be as comfortable fighting from off his back as he is sitting at a table eating his dinner. The reason? He fights from there in Newaza (ground fighting) all the time.

So our indoctrination into believing that the back position is a weak position has to change. It is/can be a very powerful position - it is the knowledge of how to fight from one's back that makes it more favourable.

There are many escapes from the back position. These are covered in-depth in *The Escapes*, and whilst they can of course be considered as 'fighting from your back' they are out of the context of this book and I would ask you to refer to the said volume for detail to complete the picture.

The beauty of fighting from your back, besides the fact that once learned you no longer harbour it as a weak position, is that it lulls the opponent into a false sense of security - he sees a finish when really there is not one there. When people see a finish they invariably rush to take it and completely forget about defending their pin (even on the pavement arena). This is where you can easily escape, or more appropriately draw them into a finishing technique.

The back position is a very strong position for barring and choking an opponent. It is also very strong for using atemi, especially eye attacks and biting. I've been on my back a few times and managed to secure a good bite that has won me the fight. This story from my book *Watch My Back* exemplifies this well, though it was very unusual. I was on my back - but

## Fighting From Your Back

in a dustbin with nothing else open for me but the bite (this was before I learned to ground fight by the way):

*It was an argument that I was not going to win and his argumentative arrogance was rapidly losing me face. I lined him up with a right and as soon as he opened his mouth again to speak, 'BANG!' I let it go. It was right on target. He stumbled off his stool, but to my astonishment he was still upright and to all intents and purposes unshaken. The shock of this paused me for a second, then I let go with a couple more punches before I was pulled off him.*

*"What was that for?" he asked, as though all I'd done was slap his face.*

*Hiding my disbelief, I said,*

*"Don't you ever try to tell me my job."*

*At this his mates dragged him out of the pub and I was left wondering why I hadn't finished the job properly. A couple of minutes later I looked outside. He was there with his mates, waiting for me. With his left hand he waved me out. Not seeing the point in delaying the inevitable I went outside.*

*"What did you hit me for?" he asked.*

*"You know why," I replied.*

*"I never done fuck all," he persisted.*

*Sensing that he was going to strike at any minute, I lined him up, hiding my preparation with,*

*"So what are you trying to say?"*

*Thinking that maybe he did just want to talk I made the mistake of hesitating and not throwing my pre-cocked punch. His right rose to serve me pennance for my mistake, but already lined up, I beat him to the punch.*

*'BANG!' Right on the button again.*

*This time he's got to go. He staggered sideways as though falling, then, again to my astonishment, he squared up and came forward. Damn that boy's got a strong jaw! I threw several punches that bounced off his head like flies off a car windscreen. I changed to the body and threw a low roundhouse to his mid-section. He came right inside as I recovered it, slowly, I'm afraid, and I felt the backs of my legs against the edge of the four foot by four foot circular, concrete rubbish bin - Oh the shame of it! I fell in backwards and was as one with yesterday's news and last night's chip packets.*

*Granite jaw, all fourteen stone of him, fell on top of me. We both exchanged blows as we struggled to get out. I almost sought sanctuary under an empty crisp packet, but a sleeping wasp had* beaten me to it. Granite, being in the enviable position of 'on top' managed to get out, but I was still stuck fast. He rained blows and insanities at me whilst his mates cheered him on. Surprisingly, even though I was losing at this point, I never felt any panic. All I needed was a foot hold and this came in the guise of his right index finger. He left it by my mouth a millisecond too long and I snapped it up. He tried to pull his finger free, so I bit it harder. I felt a popping sensation as my teeth severed his skin and the blood oozed from his finger into my mouth.

'Oh no!' I thought, 'I'm not wearing a condom!'

With his bleeding finger right in my mouth I reached out with my right hand and grabbed his testicles (as you do). Using them and him as a leverage, I prised my way out of the bin. I kept biting his finger harder and harder in an attempt at weakening him, so he might give in, but drunkenness and stubbornness made him carry on.

With my left hand I grabbed his cotton shirt to give myself better leverage and better pulling power. I double stepped back with my right foot, I kicked him straight between the legs. He still wouldn't give in. I was starting to get disheartened. Nothing that I hit him with seemed to have any effect.

# Introduction

*With his near-severed finger still in the grip of my teeth and my left hand still gripping his near ripping shirt tightly, I slightly widened my stance and bit harder on his finger to distract him from what I was about to do. As he yelled in pain I released my bite hold on the finger and pulled him rapidly towards me with both hands. At the same time thrusting my head forward, I head-butted him straight in the face, once, then twice with every ounce of energy and spirit that I could muster. He hit the ground like a concrete pillar and I thought his lights were out. But no, the strong bastard was still conscious and holding onto the shirt that he had ripped off my back as he fell - I lifted my foot in the air and stamped in his face."*

So whilst it is nice to know how to bar and choke and escape from on your back it is also worth remembering that the real bread and butter techniques are, whenever possible, the order of the day. If you look too hard for the hidden you'll miss the obvious.

In one of my fights I remember a guy catching my leg as I kicked him in the stomach with a roundhouse kick. He pushed me to the ground, still holding my left leg and probably thought that it was all over (it is now), but as I fell I spun my left hip and walloped him in the head with a right roundhouse and knocked him clean out. He actually fell on top of me. At first I didn't realise that he was out so I whacked him a couple of times more, I realised when his unconscious body rolled off me onto the floor.

So if you can damage/finish an opponent in vertical grappling, before it hits the ground all the better. The atemi will only take up a small part of this book. A poke in the eye or a punch in the face doesn't take much explaining after all, but they are very important and should receive just as much flight time as the other, more aesthetic techniques such as the choke and the arm bars.

## Note

Chokes and strangles are very dangerous, please practise with great care and always release the opponent when/as soon as he taps out. It is very easy to knock an opponent out with these techniques inadvertently. Always work under supervision so that a third party can spot when a fighter is in trouble and cannot, or does not have time to tap out. I do not recommend their use to minors.

## Review

For those who have read the other volumes of this series I apologise for repeating material. I would however like to, before I start talking about techniques from the various positions, quickly review the basic pins, because if you do not know them a lot of the speak through out the text may seem like gobble-de-gook.

I have no intention of actually going into the histrionics of the holds, how to defend and attack from them and the real intricacies etc. that, as I said, is a volume on its own. I will repeat though that the pins are the bedrock of ground fighting and to go on to finishing techniques of a complex nature before learning the imperative basics is a quick way to failing at everything that you attempt.

Master the standing and walking before you try the running and sprinting, the control of the opponent on the floor, via the pinning techniques, is so very, very, VERY important that to miss it is like diving in the water before you have learned to swim.

## Fighting From Your Back

All I will list in this chapter is the holds themselves with one accompanying illustration so that, if you haven't read the other books and have no knowledge of the 'ground' you'll at least understand the 'speak'.

## The Mount Position

## Side Mount

## Reverse Mount

# Fighting From Your Back

## The Side Four Quarter

## The Scarf Hold

# The Jack-Knife

# Reverse Scarf Hold

# Fighting From Your Back

## Upper 4 /14 Pin

# Chapter One

## The Guards
## - from the pre-mount Position

The first thing to cover in *Fighting From Your Back* is the guard positions. These enable you to control the movement of the opponent with your hands, feet and legs. It also enables you to set up some solid finishing technique either with atemi or with chokes and bars from the pre-mount position, as illus, which is when the opponent is between your legs and trying to climb to the mount position for his finish. Or he may be there simply trying to get back to his feet - the guards stop him, hopefully, from doing both.

## The Ju-Jitsu scissor Guard

I have mentioned the scissor guard throughout the series and, basically, it is when you wrap your legs around the opponent's waist to stop him from mounting you. Whilst your legs are around his waist your hands should grip his shoulders/face/head etc to keep him from climbing up and also be used to attack the opponent from the same position.

## Fighting From Your Back

Although it may seem a weak position to punch from, it is not, with practise you can really damage from here, especially with eye attacks. The opponent has the opportunity also to attack from inside the scissor guard, but he lacks the movement and leverage to really make those attacks work for him - also your hands are well placed to cover the shots with blocks and parries.

The time to bring your legs down from the scissor guard is when you see/feel the opportunity to finish or escape. If you are practised at atemi from this position you can easily finish with that alone.

If you shuffle your body backwards you can also take the Judo guard from the scissor guard by bringing your legs down and placing them on the opponent's thighs.

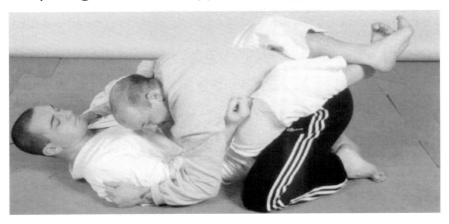

## The Judo Guard

The Judo guard is also a very strong position where you can, with practise, hold the opponent at bay for a very long time. It is best used when you catch an opponent early on in his climb to mount. Place your feet onto the opponent's thighs and your hands at his shoulders/face/head etc. to control the upper body. Use your feet to check the opponent everytime he tries to move forward. To unbalance him keep kicking his knees away so that he falls onto his face (this is a good time to turn him or bar his arm). If he gets too feisty then poke your finger into his neck, up his nose or in his eyes to control or stop him completely. You can also control the opponent very well by pushing your fingers into the gap just above his collar bone. This will discourage him from wanting to come forward.

The higher up the opponent's thighs you place your feet the easier it is to control and feel his intentions. However, if you want to push his leg/s from under him this is easier done with the foot closer to his knee. I tend to keep my feet high for control and then bring them down to the knee for attack. It is also helpful, when in the judo guard, to shuffle as far back as you can. This allows you more control, better access to finishes and escapes and inhibits the opponent's striking ability.

## Leg Turn

If the opponent lifts his left leg (or right) high to get over your legs and thus into the mount, lift your right leg high, under his knee, and force him onto his back, where you can take up the mount. Or if this is not an option and the opponent is climbing past the guard quickly wrap your legs around his waist and make the Ju-Jitsu guard.

## Knee turn

Again, if the opponent is getting past the Judo guard jam your left knee across his thighs (or right knee) to block his ascent, push his right knee from under him with your left foot so that he flattens out and quickly turn him using your right knee - go to the mount.

# Fighting From Your Back

These guards need to be isolated and practised till distraction. They are acquired techniques and a feel has to be found. Sensitivity is the name of the game with most ground fighting, not least with the guards. Once mastered they are very easy and effective techniques that use up very little fuel while, on the other hand, the opponent is using up bags of fuel to get past them.

It won't come by looking at the pictures, you need many hours of flight time just in these positions to get them off.

# Chapter Two

## Attacking from your back

### Under the mount

The art here is to stop the opponent sitting upright in the mount by grabbing his head or his arms - once upright it is very difficult to attack him and you become completely defensive. Once he is upright your best hope is to bridge him off (see *The Escapes*) or catch hold of his arm/s and pull him back down so that you can better control/attack him.

As far as the hands are concerned, from under the mount, you're wasting your time. There simply is not the distance or the leverage to reach let alone hurt him, certainly when he is sat upright. Your best bet then is biting. I have finished many times from under the mount with a bite, and while butting is unlikely to finish it will weaken the opponent. In the right position the fingers can be used to attack the eyes and pull the opponent off by placing then into the corner of the opponents mouth and ripping (*The Escapes*).

## Eye poke

Grab the opponent's right hand/arm and pull him in close, simultaneously shoot the fingers of the opposite hand into/ through his eye. Whilst this is not the easiest of attacks from this position it only takes one good shot to get the opponent off you and steal the fight.

## Fighting From Your Back

## Butt

Wherever and whenever the opportunity arises butt the opponent in the ear, nose or face, another acquired technique that will feel useless without practising from this range.

## Punch

Occasionally the opponent's face may come into range, especially when he is going from the upright mount to the defensive mount. Punch him at every given opportunity: this is a weakener as opposed to a finisher and a good ground fighter will give you no opportunity at all to punch from this position.

## Bite

This is a last resort technique, but being under the mount is a last resort position - you're already in the shit if the opponent is sitting astride your chest trying to beat you a new face. If you have the taste for it (if you'll forgive the pun) you will finish with the bite from this position everytime. Unlike the hands the teeth need no leverage, only a target.

When the opponent is in the defensive mount (if he isn't try and pull him into it) bite his ear or his face/mouth/nose/eye lids/neck etc. I need say no more, once it is on the fight is usually over. And if you are sitting there thinking that you wouldn't/couldn't/shouldn't bite - and I know that there will be a few of you - think again - what price are you willing to

# Fighting From Your Back

pay not to bite your adversary? Are you prepared to let him beat you to death? Are you prepared to let him rape you, or your wife/daughter/mother/son once he has dealt with you? Does your morality mean that much to you? I don't think so.

Think of the most precious person in your world, the one that you profess to be willing to die for (so you'll die for them but you won't bite a callous, unsolicited low life adversary for them). Even if they are not there at the time of the assault who do you think your beating/hospitalisation/death is going to affect the most, believe me it will not be you. It'll be the people in your life that love you that will bleed the most - so get real and yank yourself out of that idealistic shell and into the 21st Century.

We are dealing these days with the cruelest enemy imaginable in a society where the police openly state that the defence of the individual is not down to them, rather it is down to the individuals themselves. Look at your idols, the ancestral icons of your ryu, Musashi, Sun Tzu, Bruce Lee etc. These men spent their lives looking for techniques and concepts that could destroy an enemy in an instant. They are legendary figures and yet Musashi killed at the drop of a hat, man, woman or child, if they were a threat, Sun Tzu the same; Bruce Lee's main artillery was a lead finger strike that would blind instantly. These men, and others of their ilk took martial in its true concept, 'designed for war' and what is war? The greatest expression of violence known to man - but also bear in mind why it is there, why you use these base, ugly and evil techniques: as Sun Tzu said, 'the purpose of war is peace', the purpose of ugly technique is there for the same reason only, so that you can survive and protect your loved ones from indiscriminate attack and death.

If you are going to get into a fire fight put some bullets in your gun - or stay at home.

## From the Judo and scissor guard

I practise a lot of punching technique from this position, and gouging, and it's amazing just how much power you can get when you practise, even though at first look you'd think that there was no power to be had from such a position.

## Fighting From Your Back

You have to practise very short range punching to be effective from here. Aim straight down the centre line so that your punches have a little more distance to build up momentum. To be more destructive just open your fist and aim the same straight line attacks using your finger/s as the bullet - one good connection would/could spell the end of the fight for the opponent, and possible the end of his sight in the eye that you attack.

## Finger in mouth

Often you can lean right over and across the top of the opponent's head (with left or right hand) and reach his lip on the other side of his face. Hook your finger into the corner of his lip and tear back, hold him there whilst you punch him in the face with the other hand, or escape by turning him with the rip.

Care has always to be taken with this technique not to actually go right into his mouth. If you get bitten it is excruciatingly painful. What I always do, and I use this technique a lot, is dig my middle finger firstly into the cheek of the opponent, about a couple of cm's from the opening of his mouth, and pull. As his face turns I then hook the finger into the very corner of his mouth. This is one of the strongest techniques that I have found - once the finger is firmly hooked and pulled the fight is usually over.

In theory you'd think that, once in the mouth, the opponent could easily bite, but in practice it is nearly impossible because you rip the lip away from the teeth so biting is no longer an option.

## Fighting From Your Back

Let the practise of the former be your bedrock to finish from your back or simply to set up finishing techniques. All of the following techniques can be worked in conjunction with atemi. The same as everything else in life, if you don't practise it then you're unlikely even to remember it, let alone become proficient.

# Chapter Three

## Chokes and strangles
### from under the mount/Judo Guard/ Ju-jitsu Guard

These can be the most devastating and unsuspecting finishes of all. The opponent has already got the winning post fixed firmly in his sight and then, all of a sudden, he finds himself unexpectedly unconscious. Getting the trained ground fighter in a choke from here is not so easily done, though I have done it many times so it is effective, because he has in-built defensive measures to stop the attack. Outside the opponent is never likely to have such knowledge and his ignorance is usually his downfall.

Even if the techniques do not secure a finish they always force the opponent to move and thus open up an escape route for you to take, so they can all be used singularly or in conjunction with other moves or escapes. They can also be used, unless stipulated in the text, from under the mount, the Judo Guard or the Ju-jitsu Guard. I shall illustrate them all from under the mount, bearing in mind that they will work equally from the other positions.

## Fighting From Your Back

## Larynx grab

### (from under the mount/Judo Guard/ Ju-jitsu Guard)

This requires a good grip, which can be developed, but has been one of my bigger finishing techniques. Simply grab the opponent with either hand, preferably your strongest, round the larynx/ wind pipe, try to join your fingers up at the other side for best effect. Avoid the neck muscles, work inside them, if you get them you can squeeze all day without any effect on the opponent.

## Trap arm choke (Under the mount)

As the opponent's right arm (or left) comes down to strike or grab you parry it across to your right and pull the opponent forward so that your right arm wraps under it and around his neck, as illus. Couple your left with your right hand so that the bone of the right wrist is across the opponent's neck and squeeze both hands and arms together to make the strangle. You also have the option from here to bridge the opponent off you (see *The Escapes*).

## Figure eight choke (Under the mount)

Firstly make sure that you have pulled the opponent into the defensive mount and have him in a head lock with your right arm, across the back of his neck, joined to your right hand at the other side. Grab your right biceps (or the sleeve thereabouts) with your left hand and feed the left hand underneath the opponent's chin, across his throat. At the other side grab your right biceps (or the sleeve thereabouts) with your left hand to complete the figure eight, squeeze everything to make the choke.

# Figure eight choke
## (Under the mount-using your sleeve)

As before, firstly make sure that you have pulled the opponent into the defensive mount and have him in a head lock with your right arm, across the back of his neck, joined to your right hand at the otherside. Grab the right cuff of your coat/jumper etc. with your left hand and hold in place whilst feeding the right arm under the opponent's chin, across his throat, and join up to make the figure eight by grabbing your left biceps (or the sleeve) with your right hand. Squeeze together by pulling to the left with your left hand and pulling to your right with your right hand (still holding the sleeves of course) to make the choke.

## Cross jacket choke

**(from under the mount/Judo Guard/Ju-jitsu Guard)**

This only really works if the opponent has a jacket that you can grab. Grab the opponent's right lapel, as deeply into his neck as you can, with your right hand making sure that your palm is facing up and the thumb is into his neck and grab his left lapel further down with your left hand. In a garrotting action pull down and across to your left with the left hand and down and to your right with your right hand to make the strangle.

# Cross Collar choke

**(from under the mount/Judo Guard/ Ju-jitsu Guard)**

Again this technique needs a strong appendage, preferably a jacket, to work. Cross your hands and grab the opponents right collar with your right hand, palms down, as deeply into the neck as you can, and grab his left collar with your left hand, palm up and as deeply as you can, make the choke by scissoring your hands into his neck/throat.

## Across and around jacket choke
## (from under the mount/ Ju-jitsu Guard)

If the opponent is in the high mount position grab his right lapel, about mid way down, with your right hand and use it to pull him down. As he comes to the defensive mount pull his lapel across to your own right. Reach over his head with your left hand and feed the lapel, or any part of the opponent's upper garment, with your right hand to your left. Pull tightly with the left hand so that the lapel goes across the opponent's neck and throat to make the choke.

## Trap arm and turn
## (From under the mount)

Push the opponent's right arm across and pull him into the defensive mount, reach over his head and grab his right arm at the wrist with your left hand. Pull on his right hand with your left and push on his right elbow (or his chin) with your right hand to turn the opponent out of the mount on to his back. Take the mount position, still keeping his hand trapped, feed your right arm under and around his neck, from your right to your left. Pin his left arm still with your chest, let go of it with your left and couple your left to your right to complete the choke and squeeze, for more leverage jump onto your toes, or to the jack-knife position, and focus your weight behind the technique.

## Over under choke
## (From under the Mount/Ju-jitsu Guard)

Wrap your right arm around the opponent head, from your left to your right, and join under his chin, across his throat with your left hand. Lean back and squeeze your arms together and up.

If employing this from under the Ju-Jitsu guard grapevine your feet around the opponent's ankles and push so that he flattens out. This will help tighten the choke and stop the opponent from being able to escape.

## Broken

The same technique applies if you cannot couple the hands cleanly under the opponent's chin because his right arm is in the way of your left. In this instance break the choke by going under his arm and coupling your hands together, this is now more of a strangle that a choke and, because the grip is broken, not quite so strong, you can still quite easily KO the opponent with it all the same.

Again, if employing this from under the Ju-Jitsu guard grapevine your feet around the opponent's ankles and push so that he flattens out, this will help tighten the choke and stop the opponent from being able to escape.

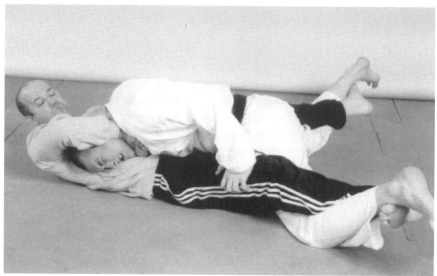

# Fighting From Your Back

## Triangular Leg Choke

**(from under the mount/Judo Guard/ Ju-jitsu Guard)**

If the opponent places his right arm between your legs in a bid to escape, quickly wrap your left leg around his neck and pull his left arm straight. This will force his shoulder against the side of his neck and form half of the choke. Wrap your left foot behind the knee of your right leg: the tighter the better, squeeze with your thighs to make the choke. If the opponent struggles punch him in the face: he'll have no defence because his arms are tied off, or poke his eyes to calm him down a little.

If the opponent, in his struggle, falls to his left or his right whilst in the leg choke don't worry, the choke will still be on, just keep on squeezing.

## Standing triangular leg choke

**(from under the mount/Judo Guard/Ju-jitsu Guard)**

If the opponent tries to stand up from the seated triangular leg choke and you cannot stop him via the atemi strike then just go with him. As he stands you will be able to place a juji Gatame arm bar, as illus., on him. Keep squeezing your thighs together to make the choke. If the opponent, in his struggle, falls to his left or his right whilst in the leg choke don't worry, the choke will still be on, just keep on squeezing.

## Seated Juji Gatame

**(From the standing triangular Leg Choke position)**

From the standing triangular leg choke you can, if you wish, take the opponent over onto his back for a seated Juji Gatame arm by un-tying your right leg from your left and bringing it in front of the opponent's face and then raking his face backwards so that he loses his balance and falls onto his back. Keep a good grip on his arm at all times. From here push the hips up and pull his arm down to make the bar.

## Reverse Juji Gatame

### (From the standing triangular Leg choke position)

If, after releasing your right leg to rake the opponent's face, he pushes (or falls) forward, instead of going backwards, allow him to fall and keep a good grip on his arm. When he lands on his belly he will already be in the reverse Juji Gatame position - from here push the hips up and pull his arm down to make the bar.

With all of these, if you want to, when the opponent tries to stop the choke, forgetting about defending his mount, you can bridge him off to escape.

Generally the ground fighting moves all flow into one another when you have practised them a lot. So if you lose one then you automatically flow into another, that's why it is best not to fight too hard for a technique, just go with the flow and there will be another one just around the corner that the opponent will force himself into.

# Chapter Four

### Chokes and strangles
### - From under the Scarf Hold

The best thing to do when you are under the scarf hold is escape, and in a hurry - it is a very vulnerable position to be in. If you can get a choke/strangle or any move on the opponent en-route that's great, but don't chase them too hard, place all your resources into actually getting out of the hold (see *The Escapes*) so that you don't get your head caved in.

Some of the escapes and chokes from this position are a little like ground chess, and, although often elongated, they will work if you know your art - note: make sure that you do otherwise just go straight for an escape.

Sometimes (actually, most times) I use attacks against the opponent's throat in the guise of chokes and strangles merely as a feint to draw them in, to get him to move or react just a little bit so that I can escape. If I manage to finish with the move, very rare from under the scarf hold, then that's a Brucie bonus.

## Right hand larynx grab

If you can get your right arm free grab the opponent's larynx and squeeze very hard, try to join your fingers up at the other side of his wind pipe. When he reacts you can also bridge him off to escape the hold.

## Naked choke

If you can get your right arm free bring it up to and past the left side of the opponent's neck so that the bone of your wrist is against his side neck muscle. Grip your own left shoulder with your right hand (either by gripping the muscle or grabbing your cloths) and wrap, as per illus, your left arm around the back of your head to make the strangle, hug tightly using your arms, chest and back muscles. This also leaves you in a good position to bridge the opponent off.

## Lapel choke

Reach over the opponent's head with your left hand and grab his furthest lapel (if your right hand is free feed the lapel to your left hand) and pull it back so that the cloth tightens across his throat to make the strangle, from here bridge to escape.

## Fighting From Your Back

## Poke, hook and leg choke

Poke under the opponent's throat with your fingers so that his head is forced back, simultaneously hook your left leg around his neck and pull him backwards so that he is now lying on his back and you are near sitting up with your leg still around his neck. Wrap your left foot around the back of your right knee and squeeze your thighs tightly to make the choke.

# Chokes and strangles - From under the Scarf Hold

**Fighting From Your Back**

## Jack-knife turn, rear mount and choke

Move your chest away from the opponent's back, simultaneously push your fingers into his face/eyes/throat etc. to force him onto his back. You will now be kneeling by his side: he'll probably still have you in a head lock. Punch him in the face so that he releases the grip and turns on to his belly, as he does mount him on his back and make the reverse mount choke.

# Chokes and strangles - From under the Scarf Hold

## Triangular Leg Choke
## from the side 4 1/4 hold down

Whilst talking about the chokes from the side 4 1/4 it is worth mentioning a good leg choke from over, as opposed to under, the hold. If the opponent has his right arm between your legs, he will often do this to try to escape. Wrap your left leg past his face and under/around his head, grip as tight as possible, and squeeze.

Be careful in practise, as this is a very powerful technique). It needs to be practised because the opponent will easily pull his head free if you do not secure it very quickly.

## Over under strangle

Wrap your right arm over the opponent's head and under his body towards his chest, make sure that the bone of the wrist runs along his side neck muscle. Feed your left arm under his body so that you can couple up with the opposite hand. Once interlinked pull tightly to make the choke, even if it does not completely secure the KO it will force the opponent to move and give you an escape route to follow.

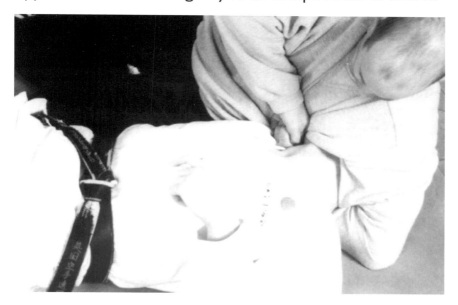

# Chapter Five

## *Bars from your back*

All of the following bars will work well especially with an opponent who is in a hurry and does not have the knowledge. Once on, these techniques, although quite innocent looking from the side lines, are joint breaking techniques that will destroy an opponent's limbs in a hurry. For this reason they are best practised with great care in the controlled arena.

### Immediate turn to Juji gatame (arm Bar)

Grip the opponent's outstretched right arm (or left) and quickly bring your left leg up and in front of his face, raking it back so that he is forced onto his back, your left foot will now be at the left (far) side of his head. At the same time bring your right leg to the right side of his head ensuring that, at all times, you keep control of his right arm. Lie onto your back and trap the opponent's head with your left leg, simultaneously wedge your right foot underneath his body at his right hand side. His arm is between your legs, pull down on his arm and push up with your hips to complete the bar. If, when you bring your foot in front of the opponent's face he forces you forward, go with the flow and as you land on your belly take the reverse Juji Gatame.

## Reverse Juji Gatame (from the Judo Guard)

Push the opponent's left leg from under him with your left foot; as he flattens out bring your left leg in front of his face and roll onto your belly to take the reverse Juji gatame.

If he tries to sit up, rake his face backwards with your left foot and force him onto his back where you can make the standard Juji Gatame by pulling down on his arm and pushing up with your hips. If he tries to stand up then you can take the standing juji gatame or rake his face with your foot and force him over onto his back for juji gatame or if he falls onto his face again then re-take the reverse juji gatame.

## Fighting From Your Back

## Standing Juji gatame

If the opponent tries to stand up from inside one of your guards, grip his right hand at the wrist with both your hands and pull it straight as he stands. Bring your left leg in front of his face and bar the arm across your hip. As per usual - if he falls forward take the reverse Juji Gatame, or rake his face so that he falls onto his back and take the seated Juji gatame.

## Failed Right Juji Gatame to left reverse Juji gatame

Although a little complex I have used this move on several occasions to finish an opponent. It's a bit complicated, though simple when you know how, so stick with it.

This is best used when you have gone for the right arm bar (or the opposite way) and the opponent tries to escape by trying to turn into you, (it's hard to actually explain so follow the illustrations). As he feeds his left arm over to try and climb through turn onto your right side and simultaneously let go of his right hand and grab his left, as soon as you have his left hand firmly gripped whip your right leg over his head and force him onto his belly and make the reverse Juju gatame.

# Fighting From Your Back

# Chapter Six

## *Finger and wrist locks*

Finger and wrist locks are rainy day techniques that I do not chase, from the vertical position I find them worse than useless (unless of course my opponent is compliant and lets me put them on). On the ground however they are pretty useful, sometimes brilliant, but I only take them when they are offered, when a bigger technique has been blocked and I need pain distraction, or occasionally to break a strong hold that may have been placed upon me by the opponent. I have won fights in the controlled arena with these techniques because when they are on the opponent either taps out or gets the bone broken. Don't place too much stock on them however, your bread and butter techniques are the bigger bars, chokes and pummelling atemi.

I will list these techniques in no particular order, if the opportunity arises then take it.

## Outside Wrist twist

Place both of your thumbs at the back of the opponents right (or left) hand between his two middle knuckles, the fingers of both your hands meeting at the centre of his palm which is facing inward. Sharply twist his wrist back and to your left.

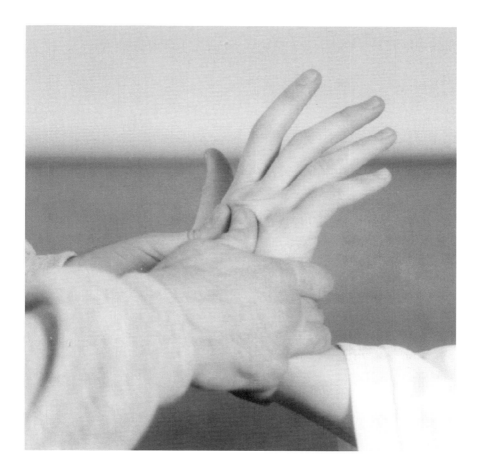

## Little finger bend

Grab the opponent's little finger and bend it to any un-natural angle until he taps out, it snaps or it releases the grip that he has on you.

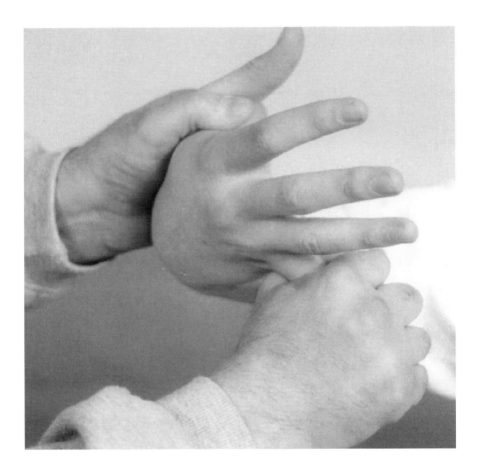

## Two finger spread

Grip two of the opponent's left fingers (may be reversed) in each of your hands (from any position that allows) and slowly (fast if you want to beak the fingers) spread and separate the fingers.

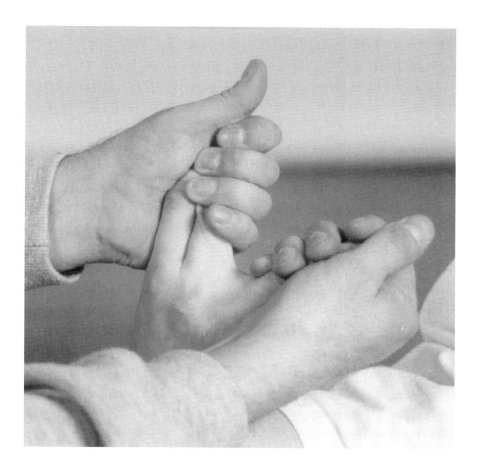

## Thumb Bend

Grab the opponent's thumb and pull it back as far as you can.

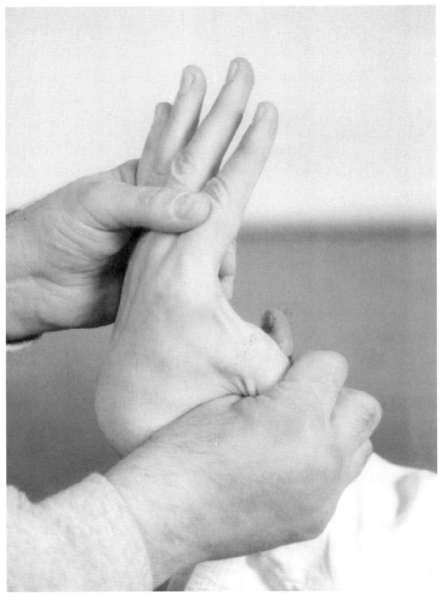

## Thumb Crush

Grab the opponent's thumb (left or right) and bend it so that

his inside tip presses against his own palm, squeeze tightly.

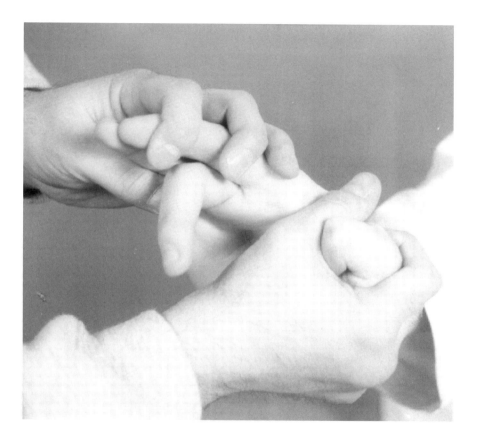

## Finger Crush

Grab at least three of the opponent's fingers (on one hand) and fold them into the palm of his own hand so that his finger nails are forced against the base of his fingers.

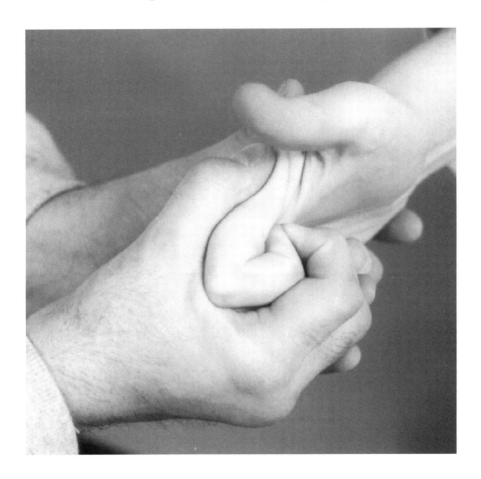

## The wrist flex

Whenever the possibility presents itself bend the opponent's wrist so that the palm is forced toward the inner surface of his forearm.

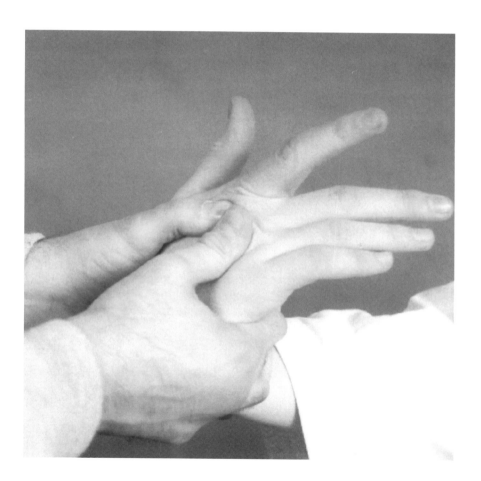

# Chapter Seven

## *Drilling*

Here are a selection of drills to practise so that you can perfect the movements herein. I repeat it in nearly every book (and I'm fed up of repeating it) drilling is where it's at. This is where technique is born and perfect technique is developed, it's amazing what you will find after drilling a technique several thousand times.

I don't want to list every technique that can be drilled and how they can be drilled because they can, and should, all be drilled till distraction. I will just list a few of the ones that I practise and leave you to make a few of your own. If you want to make a technique your own, isolate it and drill it, not forgetting that, once learned, they should all be pressure tested. This is another vital, probably the most vital aspect of acquiring a technique.

When I was training in Thai, I was struggling to get one of the more complex double steps that they so favour, so, I went out to practise it at a local park. Along the side of the park was a dirt track that led, seemingly, to nowhere, I guess it must have been about a quarter of a mile long. After warming up I stood at the start of this track and did my double step from one end to the other, bearing in mind that each techniques carried me about the distance of one normal walking step.

I didn't go crazy, I did some full speed and others slow for technique. At the end of the track I took a rest, had a stretch and then did the same all the way back. When I got to the beginning again (it was dark by then) I had got the technique, it was mine, it wasn't as good as I would get it with more polishing but I did have it and have never lost it to this day.

On another occasion when I wanted to perfect my Osoto gari throw (major reap) I went to the same park very early in the morning and chose a suitable tree (the local dogs were none to happy) where I practised, one hundred techniques in a row each side, my Osoto, it was one of the most tiring sessions of my life but, again, it gave me mass flight time in a very short space of time. I have to warn you though that some of these sessions have taken me beyond my own limits and made me ill, the price I had to pay, which is probably not a always a good thing. So in a book of this nature it would not perhaps be very sensible of me to recommend the same. What I do recommend however is that you do drill, and drill more than other people are prepared to if you want to be better than them.

## Punching from your back

Have your opponent kneel in your scissor guard holding a pair of focus pads, from your back punch up at the pads as hard as you can, the power will come with each practise session. Also hold one of the pads, as though it were the opponent's head, and punch repeatedly with the other hand, then change to the other side. Work in two or three minute rounds for five rounds each.

## Cross lapel choke

Practice the cross lapel choke from the scissor guard, try and practise rapidly from the left side to the right side to get your hands used to the position and to finding the right spot quickly. 50 reps each side.

## Figure eight choke

Practise the left and the right side to this technique, again getting the movement quicker each time so that eventually your hands just fall into place. 25 reps each side.

## Triangular leg choke

Wrap your right leg around the opponent's neck in preparation and then throw your left leg over the right foot and then back to the floor again - do 50 reps as quickly and as smoothly as possible, then change to the other side. This is also a very good neck exercise because during practise the head is constantly lifted off the floor.

## Poke and hook leg choke
## (from under the scarf hold)

Poke and hook the opponent's head with your left leg and quickly tie off with the opposite leg to make the leg choke. Lie straight back down under the scarf hold position and repeat the movement, each time trying to get smoother and faster, 25 reps each side.

## Immediate turn to Juji gatame (from the Judo Guard)

Grab the opponent's arm and hook your left leg over and in front of his face, rake it down and make Juji gatame then go straight back to the guard position and repeat the movement to the opposite side. 25 reps each side.

## Reverse Juji Gatame (from the Judo guard)

Grab the opponent's right hand/arm with both your hands. Push the opponent's left leg from under him with your right foot and whip your left foot over his head to make reverse Juji Gatame. Return quickly to the start position and do the same to the opposite side. 25 reps each side.

## The pendulum

From standing Juji gatame take the opponent forward and down to the ground and make reverse Juji Gatame. Let the opponent stand up, still holding his arm and take him on to his back and make a straight Juji gatame, then go back to the standing arm bar and, again, take the reverse arm bar. Go up and down in a pendulum motion for 25 five reps.

# Conclusion

That is the end of *Fighting From your Back*. Place it in the jigsaw with the other sections to complete the picture. Don't just talk the talk and read the words and look at the pictures, take the techniques into the training arena where they can be forged ready for the pavement arena.

Read the books again and again, when you can pick the books up and find a technique you have not perfected then that is the time to move on and find more information from different sources. Every time one book of knowledge closes, another full of new information and new techniques opens, that's the exciting thing about the martial arts, it's a never ending journey of discovery and self discovery.

Read as much as you can, watch as many videos on training as you can also, small libraries make great men. I have books in my collection from the 1800's about men and women, such as you and I, who were on the same journey as we are now. Their journey has ended and now it is our turn to take the wheel of discovery; life can be very short, so seize every moment as though it were your last - it may well be - and gather the knowledge in like a summer harvest.

It's an exciting world with so much information and so many wonderful teachers willing, wanting, to pass it on - you've just got to make the effort where others do not and seek them out, knowledge is power.

I hope that this volume has helped you in your search, thank you for taking the time to read and learn.

**Other books in this series:**

# GEOFF THOMPSON'S GROUND FIGHTING SERIES

# PINS: THE BEDROCK

GROUND FIGHTING

# GEOFF THOMPSON

SUMMERSDALE

GEOFF THOMPSON'S GROUND FIGHTING SERIES

# THE ESCAPES

GROUND

# GEOFF
# THOMPSON

SUMMERSDALE

# GEOFF THOMPSON'S GROUND FIGHTING SERIES

# CHOKES AND STRANGLES

## GEOFF THOMPSON

SUMMERSDALE

GEOFF THOMPSON'S GROUND FIGHTING SERIES
ARM BARS & JOINT LOCKS
GROUND FIGHTING
GEOFF THOMPSON
SUMMERSDALE

# GEOFF THOMPSON'S GROUND FIGHTING SERIES

# FIGHTING FROM YOUR KNEES

## GEOFF THOMPSON

SUMMERSDALE

www.geoffthompson.com

www.summersdale.com